*Travis Barker, MPA GCPM*
*Innovate Vancouver*
*consulting@innovatevancouver.org*
*www.innovatevancouver.org*

*Ordering Information:*
*Quantity sales. Special discounts are available on quantity purchases by corporations, associations, and others. For details, contact the publisher at the address above.*

*Disclaimer*

The information provided within this book is for general informational purposes only. While we try to keep the information up-to-date and correct, there are no representations or warranties, express or implied, about the completeness, accuracy, reliability, suitability or availability with respect to the information, products, services, or related graphics contained in this eBook for any purpose.

# Table of Contents

In a value based service setting the positive behavior support methodology has responded to the call for a safe, respectful, and evidence informed practice for responding to challenging behaviors. Instead of managing or treating behaviors, the positive behavior support methodology seeks to replace the goal seeking behavior with strategies that are more productive. The response of the service and healthcare fields to this approach has been overwhelming; with legislation, organizational policies, research, educational curriculum, and communities of care all responding in support.

Positive behavior support has been described in the quote below

> *"Positive Behavior Support (PBS) is a process for understanding and resolving the problem behavior of children that is based on values and empirical research. It offers an approach for developing an understanding of why the child engages in problem behavior and strategies for preventing the occurrence of problem behavior while teaching the child new skills. Positive behavior support offers a holistic approach that considers all factors that impact on a child and the child's behavior. It can be used to address problem behaviors that range from aggression, tantrums, and property destruction to social withdrawal."*

Source: Fox, L., & Duda, M. A. (n.d.). Complete Guide to Positive Behavior Support.

The following pages provide an overview of the positive behavior support methodology. The first section identifies beliefs often presented staff, and the corresponding (or dissonant) beliefs realized by support models (such as PBS) and further exploration. Understanding these patterns can help staff to better identify what strategies are helpful and what outcomes are desired. The second section that follows provides a brief overview of additional client beliefs and the staff strategies that can be used in these scenarios. As with all positive behavior support plans the strategy is individualized identified, and varies per client, based on the skills currently being used and the goals desired by the client.

The third section provides a brief overview of how to use questions and their contextual point of reference, to explore specific scenarios, beliefs, or issues. Questions are considered one of the tools of choice within the positive behavior support methodology. This is because questions help to gather information and narrative directly from the client regarding what they find meaningful, their intent, experience, and the goals being pursued. Staff can then use this information to formulate the best strategies to use, based on the client's current skill repertoire, presentation, and other situational variables.

The fourth section provides a brief overview of context based points of references. Further quantitative and descriptive language is identified to evaluate strategies and outcome to capture the clinical presentation observed. This shared language, and metrics, helps to maintain alignment and coordination amongst the client stakeholders and care team members. The fifth section provides a brief overview of the 'antecedent' model which seeks to identify the situation, skills, and intended goals that existed prior to the behavioral event occurring. Understanding these antecedents is crucial towards helping the care team to identify best practices and strategies to support the client.

The sixth section provides a generic ABC (antecedent-behavior-consequence) tracking form that can be modified and tailored for your client. Tracking the frequency, location, and antecedents to specific behaviors helps the care team to evaluate client goals as well as the effectiveness of staff strategies. The seventh section provides a graphic model of a generic 'positive behavior support' approach.

The eighth section provides a generic example of a functional behavioral assessment and positive behavior support plan. The details in this example are generic and do not represent a real person. The document flows from issue identification to evaluation, assessment, planning, and ends with the goals with suggested metrics.

The ninth and tenth sections include guidelines for writing positive behavior support plans, and conducting functional behavior assessment (which are used to develop the PBSP). These guidelines are written into the DDA 5.14 legislation in Washington State, and so represent an example of how significantly the PBS methodology has been embraced.

**Using the PBS Approach as an Evaluating & Planning Framework**

This Positive Behavior Support Guidelines are not intended to be exhaustive as the approach is to be significantly individualized for the client's needs, skills, goals, and the setting in which the approach is to be implemented. It is particularly true that there is 'no one size fits all' approach to behavioral intervention, but the PBSP framework, methods, and tools represent an evidence based practice for identifying, evaluating, and planning the care team's response.

The strategies employed in a positive behavior support plan share a common emphasis on replacing dysfunctional strategies with functional ones. Although ABA is the most often cited model for designating follow up behavioral strategies there are other social, psychological, and medical models needed to support the overall wellbeing of the client. A positive behavior support plan (PBSP) does not just emphasize acute behavior but also focuses on supporting all of the life domains.

# Staff Beliefs & Client Perceptions of Helpfulness

This section identifies beliefs often presented staff, and the corresponding (or dissonant) beliefs realized by support models (such as PBS) and further exploration. The third column provides examples of key principles or framing points of references that can be used when responding to, and in order to explore, an event. Understanding these patterns can help staff to better identify what strategies are helpful and what outcomes are desired.

## Group Activity:

*As a group discuss the issue of how staff beliefs influence strategies used and their results.*

*On a whiteboard identify suggestions to overcome the limitations (and challenges) of using inflexible beliefs.*

*Discuss the suggested principles identified for developing useful interventions.*

*Discuss the ABA antecedent-consequence chain of analysis*

| Question | Staff Believe | But research finds that......... | Principles to Guide Staff Interventions |
|---|---|---|---|
| Cause | Each behavior is the cause of what follows it | Cause precedes the problem, but this does not say when the cause occurred or why | Cause can be obvious or implied. Cause can be the larger pattern or a specific incident. Cause can be perception or a physical event. |
| Self-Control | The client has control over their behavior | The client has had this behavior for many years | Self-control is learned and not an absolute skill everyone has. Self-control has to be taught. Self-control has to be prioritized. Self-control may conflict with other priorities. |

| | | | |
|---|---|---|---|
| Right vs Wrong | Staff are doing the right thing to help the client | The client does not feel it is helpful | *Right is defined as what is perceived as helpful and right by the client. Sometimes right is not helpful. Sometimes what is perceived as wrong is helpful. Right vs. wrong is an oversimplification.* |
| Helping | Responding to the behavior will help it stop | Will not replace the behaviors use | *Reacting to a situation does not help replace the behavior in the future.* |
| Being polite | I was polite and could not have made the situation worse | The situation escalated anyhow, thus…. | *Being polite can also be perceived as condescending, belittling, avoidant, fearful; being polite can also include behavior that is passive and unresponsive; being polite does not mean you are using others skills that are appropriate.* |
| Protecting | I should be protecting the other clients | When done publicly this is experienced as rejecting and confrontational; escalating behaviors | *Protecting can be done privately and does not have to be done in a way that is experienced as confrontational or antagonistic.* |
| Patience | If I leave the client alone they will calm down and things will be fine | This feels like avoidance and ignoring; which feels like punishment. The client gets paranoid. | *If the client does not have the skills to deal with the situation this will not improve by leaving them alone.* |
| Relationships | If I am friendly, inclusive, and supportive everything will be fine | If what I am doing is not experience as friendly, inclusive, and supportive than it really is not the right strategy | *A healthy relationship and lifestyle is built collaboratively with the client on their terms (when appropriate).* |

# Client Beliefs & Staff Strategies to be Helpful

The second section provides a brief overview of additional client beliefs and the staff strategies that can be used in these scenarios. The third column provides examples of key principles or framing points of references that can be used when responding to an event. As with all positive behavior support plans the strategy is individualized identified, and varies per

**Group Activity:**

*As a group discuss the issue of how client beliefs influence the strategies they use and their results.*

*On a whiteboard identify suggestions to help the client overcome (and challenge) the limitations of using inflexible beliefs. The goal is to help the client replace ineffective behaviors with effective behaviors.*

*Discuss the suggested principles for developing useful interventions based on the identified function of the behavior.*

| *Question* | The Client Believes | But Staff often Realize that...... | Principles to Guide Staff Interventions |
|---|---|---|---|
| *Comparing* | If staff do not compare me to others I'll be fine | Negative comparisons are not the same as positive comparisons (you do well just like....) | *Use positive interventions, not negative interventions. Use goals to motivate instead of comparisons.* |
| *Religion* | If staff do not talk religion with me when upset I'll be fine | Religion is experienced as positive and empowering when I am not upset; when I do not like this topic it is not due to religion, but my relationships with others at the time. | *Use religion as something to build the relationship when the client is not in crisis; avoid the use of religion as a topic* |
| *Inclusion* | If staff try to include me in things I'll be fine | I push others away and so others leave me alone; I do not | *Include in advance, not last minute. Last minute inclusion, while* |

|  | | | |
|---|---|---|---|
| | | feel included, but this is sometimes due to my own choices | *intending to be supportive, is often experienced as bossy and inconsistent with the client's lifestyle (priorities for the day)* |
| *Listening* | If staff listen to me I'll be fine | I have great difficulty recognizing when others are listening to me; listening does not require that someone agrees with me, although this is often what I insist on | *Listening is two-way. Support two way listening by role planning that you hear them, that you appreciate being heard, and that the mutual understanding reach is very helpful.* |
| *Supporting* | If staff support me I'll be fine | I have great difficulty recognizing when others are supporting me; I can be fickle, and my preferences change constantly, making it difficult for others to support me AND for me to feel supported (because I do a lot of testing of others to verify if they care about me) | *Feeling supported requires being willing to accept support. Confirm you are trying to provide support, ask if you are being helpful, ask for suggestions about how to be more helpful; if necessary, explain that you are sorry that your attempt to be helpful is not helpful at 'this' time but you will try harder* |
| *Helping others* | I am just trying to help the girls; staff are not letting me | I have difficulty recognizing when I am not being helpful | *Identifying when we are not helpful requires knowing when others are upset, are not responding to our help, when we are negatively responding to others refusal to accept our help, and understanding when we should let others step in* |
| *Being allowed to help* | I am just trying to be helpful; I'll be fine as long as I am allowed to help | I do not always have the skills to be helpful; so when I am not perceived as being helpful I get | *Acknowledge that you recognize the client is being helpful; validate every time you observe the client identifying* |

| | | | |
|---|---|---|---|
| | | upset and make things worse and escalate. I in turn get more upset. | *that their strategy is not helpful; also reinforce every time the client asks you to help them be helpful, or for you to step in and take care of the situation.* |
| Relationships | I just want to be loved | I have difficulty loving myself; as a result I go through a lot of effort testing others to help me identify if they 'truly' care about me; but what I am actually doing is pushing others away and creating an interaction that does not feel loving | *Validate activities that the client values. Validate positive skills used by the client. Reinforce achievements. Reinforce positive self-beliefs. Include in decisions, choices, and opportunities. Create opportunities for 1:1 activities with staff.* |

# Evaluating Cause & Effect: Using Questions to Explore Antecedents

This section provides a brief overview of how to use questions (column 2) and their contextual point of reference (column 1), to explore specific scenarios, beliefs, or issues. Questions are considered one of the tools of choice within the positive behavior support methodology. This is because questions help to gather information and narrative directly from the client regarding what they find meaningful, their intent, experience, and the goals being pursued. Staff can then use this information to formulate the best strategies to use, based on the client's current skill repertoire, presentation, and other situational variables.

**Group Activity:**

*As a group discuss event specific factors that influence how we analyze, evaluate, and identify issues and their solutions.*

*On a whiteboard list the reasons why you think a flexible and adaptive approach is required to respond to problem behaviors.*

*Discuss how the methodology supports flexibility and why this is important.*

| Principles for Staff Interventions: Asking Questions in an Effort to Identify Trends and Solutions | |
|---|---|
| *Cause* | Is the cause limited to this event? Or related to a general pattern of events? Is the cause related to what can be seen? Or what is perceived? Emotion? Interaction elsewhere? Unexpressed need? |
| *Self-Control* | Is the client able to provide self-control over this behavior regularly? Is self-control assumed or proven? Does the client have the skills for self-control? Do they have the support for self-control? |
| *Right vs Wrong* | Who is identifying what is right? Wrong? Is wrong a general statement or specific? Is the definition of right shared by the client? Do you and the client have the same priorities? If not, why? |
| *Helping* | What does the client want? What would they consider helpful? Are they finding your efforts helpful? If not, why? What additional skills are needed to be helpful? Are your strategies flexible? |
| *Being polite* | Is your attempt to be 'polite' an active or passive behavior? Avoidant or engaging behavior? Is your attempt to be 'polite' also maintaining healthy boundaries? |
| *Protecting* | Does the client need protecting? Is your attempt to 'protect' others a private or public strategy? Is safety an issue? If not, does your strategy to 'protect' push others away? |

| | |
|---|---|
| *Patience* | Is being 'patient' active or passive? Does being 'patient' involve maintaining healthy boundaries? Is being patient avoiding or engaging? |
| *Relationships* | Does the client consider the relationship you have with them to be positive? If not, why? Does the relationship you have with the client help support healthy boundaries? If not, why? |
| *Comparing* | Are you comparing against others who are perceived as doing better? Can you compare skills they have used in the past and would benefit from using now? |
| *Religion* | Are you using relation to identify behaviors that the client should pursue but is not currently using? Could you identify behaviors that they are using that are helpful? And build upon them? |
| *Inclusion* | Are you including on your schedule or on the client's schedule? Are you including in things the client values? Or that you value? Are you including with planning in advance? Or last minute? |
| *Listening* | Are you agreeing or disagreeing? Are you asking for consensus? Or building consensus? Are you validating what you agree with? Confirming that you hear their concerns? |
| *Supporting* | Are you supporting your goals or their goals? Do you agree on common goals or are you pursuing conflicting goals? Does the client know you are supporting? If not, why? |
| *Helping others* | Are you helping everyone or only a few? Is your attempt to help many people at the same time experienced as rejecting by others? Could you have more help from coworkers to help others? |
| *Being allowed to help* | Is your approach effective? Do you need help "to help"? What skills are you using to help? What skills do you need to develop in order to help more? Do you coworkers have strategies to borrow? |
| *Relationships* | Are you supporting everyone or only one person in the relationship? Are you supporting healthy boundaries or unhealthy boundaries? Are you providing ongoing or only incremental support? |

## Evaluating Cause & Effect: Descriptions & Metrics

This section provides a brief overview of context based points of references (column 1). Further quantitative and descriptive language is identified to evaluate strategies and outcome to capture the clinical presentation observed (column 2). This shared language, and metrics, helps to maintain alignment and coordination amongst the client stakeholders and care team members.

### Group Activity:

As a group discuss the basic principles needed to identify causes and solutions to ineffective (and challenging) behaviors.

How are principles more helpful then using the same strategy every time?

Discuss and identify the function of a behavior

| | **Principles for Staff Interventions: Breaking Down Our Assumptions and Recognizing the Complexity of Events** |
|---|---|
| *Cause* | Past, or Present; Observed, or Not Observed; Perceived, or Known; |
| *Self-Control* | Assumed, or Proven; Capable, or Not Capable; |
| *Right vs Wrong* | Right, or Wrong; Wrong, or Right; For the Group, or the Individual; for this Event, or for Always; For you, or for Them; |
| *Helping* | Helping, or Not Helping; Your Definition, or Their Definition; What You Are Willing to Do, or What They Want You to Do; |
| *Being polite* | Being Polite, or Being Rude; Being Polite According to You, or According to Them; |
| *Protecting* | Protecting Them, or You; Protecting One of Them, or All of Them; Protecting Respectfully, or Protecting Disrespectfully; Protecting Publically, or Protecting Privately; |
| *Patience* | Patience, or Avoidance; Patience, or Not Responding; Patience, or Ignoring; Patience, or Ambivalence; |
| *Relationships* | Your Relationship, or Their Relationship; Others Relationship, or Their Relationship; Group Expectations, or Your Expectations; Individual Expectations, or Group Expectations; |
| *Comparing* | Comparing to what You Value, or what They Value; What others are achieving, or what They Have Achieved; |

| | |
|---|---|
| *Religion* | Your Religion, or Their Religion; On Your Schedule, or On Their Schedule; Based on Your Values, or Their Values; |
| *Inclusion* | Including On Your Schedule, or On Their Schedule; Including in Activities You Value, or They Value; Including in a Few Activities, or All Activities; Last Minute, or Planning in Advance; |
| *Listening* | Listening, or Understanding; Agreeing, or Disagreeing; Validating, or Invalidating; Sharing, or Hiding; Learning, or Assuming; |
| *Supporting* | Seeking to Support, or to be Supported; Supporting, or Influencing; Influencing, or Stopping; |
| *Helping others* | Helping others, Versus Trying to Pacify the Situation; Helping to Solve the Immediate Problem, or Helping Build the Skills so the Future Recurrence of the Same Problem is Handled Differently; |
| *Being allowed to help* | Accepting Help from Others, or Requiring Others Help You; Accepting Help, or Pushing Others Away (implicitly indicating I want help but refusing it at the same time); |
| *Relationships* | A Relationship on My Terms, or Their Terms; A Relationship that is Meaningful to Me, or to Them; A Relationship that is Improving, or Static; Building Relationship Skills, or Using Static Skills; |

This section provides a brief overview of the 'antecedent' model which seeks to identify the situation, skills, and intended goals that existed prior to the behavioral event occurring. Six contextually based terms of reference are identified (column 1) followed by principles to guide their elaboration (column 2). The perception of a pattern should not be taken for granted but instead should be explored further in order to better understand the event. Understanding these antecedents is crucial towards helping the care team to identify best practices and strategies to support the client.

## Group Activity:

As a group discuss the basic principles needed to identify causes and solutions to ineffective (and challenging) behaviors.

How are principles more helpful then using the same strategy every time?

Discuss the methodology to identify the function of a behavior

| | Principles to Identify Causes and Solutions: Using a Flexible and Adaptive Approach |
|---|---|
| Events | Are not always isolated to a single event. Some are Trends. |
| Trends | Are not always observable. Escalation gets worse if the problem is ignored. |
| Cause | Is not always obvious. May be psychological and not environmental and/or physical. |
| Responsibility | Is not always isolated. May involve several people, or everyone. Escalations can be additive. |
| Solutions | Is not always time limited. May require days or weeks. |
| Intervention | Is not always effective on the first try. May require training, behavior replacement, environmental changes, or further analysis (FBA). |

This section provides a generic ABC (antecedent-behavior-consequence) tracking form that can be modified and tailored for your client. Tracking the frequency, location, and antecedents to specific behaviors helps the care team to evaluate client goals as well as the effectiveness of staff strategies. Most ABC style tracking forms focus on documenting incidents, staff response, the trigger, time & location of the event, and people involved. Additional sections or questions can be added to your team's tracking form, as needed.

## Antecedent Behavior Consequence Analysis Form (ABC)

**Participant Name:**_____

__

**Instructions: Complete in full. Use ink.**
**You may use abbreviations.**

**Incidents:**

a. Nightmares
b. pounding in anger
c. denting things
d. holes in walls due to pounding
e. holes in walls due to tools
f. damaging other's property
j. Yelling verbal assaults
g. damaging own property
h. Instigating and assaulting others
k. other: _____

i. instigated by others and assaulting them

**Intervention Response**

I. Team Conference
II. Re-teach expectations
III. Separation
IV. Peer mediation
V. Recovery in room
VI. Recovery Outside.
VII. Attend Outing
VIII. Help Calm Down
IX. Speak with staff on phone
X. Distraction
XI. Delay of outing
XII. Verbal Cue
XIII. Extra time spent on task
XIV. Exercise
XV. Problem Solve
XVI. Other_____ _____

| The antecedent is the most important | Antecedent/ Trigger- | Behavior code- Also briefly describe | How did staff intervene and what |
|---|---|---|---|

| information | What happened, or what was going on just prior? | what the behavior looked like | was the outcome? |
|---|---|---|---|
| Time:<br><br>Date:<br><br>Staff Signature: | | | |
| Time:<br><br>Date:<br><br>Staff Signature: | | | |
| Time:<br><br>Date:<br><br>Staff Signature: | | | |
| Time:<br><br>Date:<br><br>Staff Signature: | | | |
| Time:<br><br>Date:<br><br>Staff Signature: | | | |

| | | | |
|---|---|---|---|
| **Time:**<br><br>**Date:**<br><br>**Staff Signature:** | | | |
| **Time:**<br><br>**Date:**<br><br>**Staff Signature:** | | | |

# The Positive Behavior Support Model

This section provides a graphic model of a generic 'positive behavior support' approach. Data collection and testing of assumptions and strategies becomes crucial. Utilizing this assess, plan, respond, and evaluate framework the care team is better equipped to evaluate their strategies and adjust when needed.

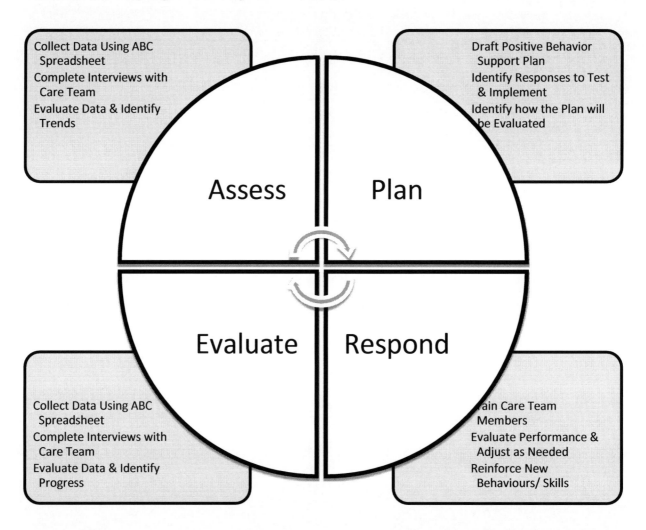

Utilizing the A-B-C model to evaluate events the care team is able to iterative upon additional lessons learned. As one strategy, and corresponding assumption, is proven ineffective the care team can revisit the situation over and over, adjusting their strategy as incremental improvements are realized.

Conducting a functional assessment (using the ABC model) requires gathering information from all sources and stakeholders in order to identify patterns. This is because a behavior may be context dependent, only surfacing when specific environments, triggers, goals, or individuals are present. Understanding these differentiating factors can help greatly in determining best practices going forward.

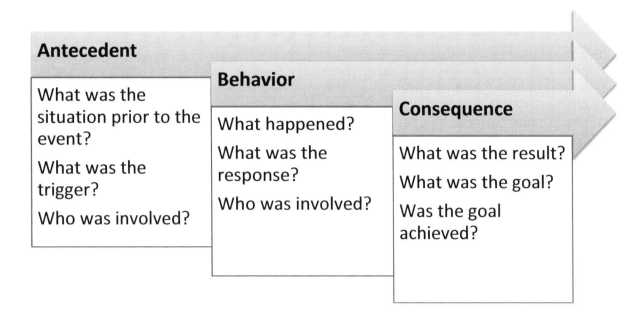

The model depicted above is actually iterative and not linear. After the consequences of one response cycle have been evaluated the care team moves on to the antecedent and data evaluation stage again. Because most first responses miss the target the care team will typically engage in a process of revaluation and pivoting as new lessons are acquired and additional strategies are explored.

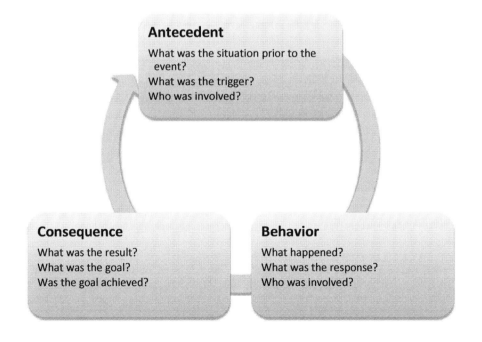

# Example: A Positive Behavior Support Plan & Functional Assessment

This section provides a generic example of a functional behavioral assessment and positive behavior support plan. The details in this example are generic and do not represent a real person. The document flows from issue identification to evaluation, assessment, planning, and ends with the goals with suggested metrics.

## Functional Assessment – Section 1

### DESCRIPTION AND PERTINENT HISTORY:

#### History:

Jennifer moved to an Agency supported home a history of unsuccessful placements at her parents/guardian's home and an adult residential center. Jennifer continues to require more support than alternative settings could provide to include medication management, Activities for Daily Living development & skill building, hygiene management, and housing case management to insure her quality of life is acceptable, housing is stable, and she is not taken advantage of.

Jennifer benefits from living with housemates who are able engage her in more activities outside of the house, support/co -pursue weight management goals, help her develop balanced and healthy relationships, and help her to learn how to better cope with stressful situations.

Jennifer's parents have obtained a doctor's order placing strict limits on Jennifer's access to food. Steps will be taken to ensure that any extension of this restriction to her new home in a supported living setting complies with the relevant policies, and that the impact on potential roommates is minimized (provided of course that the roommates do not have the same doctor-ordered restriction placed upon them).

Jennifer tends to be quite flirty in public with both familiar and unfamiliar people. Jennifer reports to have as many as 2-3 boyfriends at a given time and has been observed to be quite receptive to flirtatious overtures by others (including at a memorial service held during 2011).

#### Quality of Life:

Jennifer currently lives in a home in Johnstonville, PA whom she shares with one housemate (two housemates possible in the household). Jennifer enjoys the staff that support on a daily basis with medication management, housing case management, activities support, ADL skill development, housing care, and social skills.

Jennifer enjoys watching movies, volunteering at the horse ranch, going to the mall, taking rides with staff and the house, going for short walks, working out at the JFDQ, visiting her family, helping with meal preparation, going to the library, sending email, looking at pictures of horses on her computer/internet, reading novels, playing board games, attending community events, and attending summer camp.

## Health/Medical/Mental Health:

Jennifer has several areas of concern with her mental health and medical health. Jennifer has obsessive compulsive picking of her skin and this is typically in the area of her breasts or her arms or scalp. She often chooses areas which are not visible to staff and requires visual checks by her support staff to make sure the open sores do not become infected.

Jennifer compulsively pulls out the hair on top of her head and both the picking and hair pulling are frequently signs of the onset of depression. Jennifer often refuses to shower and requires prompting frequently to complete daily hygiene tasks. Jennifer has a restriction to food access as she tends to binge eat. Jennifer has an 1800-calorie per day dietary restriction from her physician. The topics of weight, food, picking, medications, and employment can be sensitive topics for Jennifer, sometimes producing resistance and avoidance.

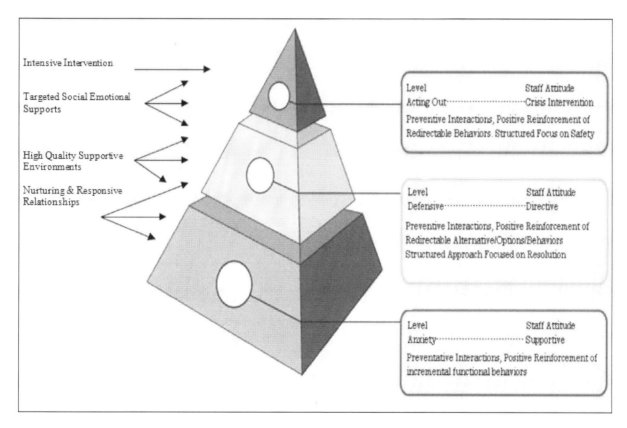

Crisis Intervention Institute, Inc, (2005). Participant Workbook for the Nonviolent Crisis Intervention Training Program: Care, Welfare, Safety, Security. Brookfield, WI: CPI.

*Martha (March 2008). What's up? Newsletter. Retrieved September 1, 2009, from Nebraska's Early Childhood Training Center Web site: http://ectc.nde.ne.gov/whatsup/2007-2008/Mar08/promising_csefel.htm*

The following sections are structured according to the escalation cycle/continuum depicted above. The strategies identified are frequently shared amongst stages. The subsequent strategies identified are not rigidly limited to any specific stage of the escalation cycle.

- The **Anxiety-Supportive** Level represents when Jennifer is presenting with no observable frustration or its correlating coping strategies/behavioral acting out.
- The **Defensive-Directive** Level represents the next stage of the escalation cycle in which Jennifer's frustration is observable but it has not yet escalated to behavioral acting-out.
- The **Acting Out-Crisis Intervention** stage represents when Jennifer has begun to physically act out beyond verbal yelling.

**Functional Assessment – Section 2**

**DEFINITION OF CHALLENGING BEHAVIOR(S)**

| |
| --- |
| **Challenging Behavior #1 – Food Theft & Binging** |
| **Definition:** Jennifer is on a physician restricted 1800 calorie per day diet and the guardians and Jennifer have established the goal to lose weight within the next year.<br><br>**Severity:** Jennifer will eat large quantities of food, hide food in her room, perseverate on the topic of food, eat food that has been discarded, and steal food from other's rooms when there is access. Jennifer will ask for food from housemates, hide food in her room, spend her entire allowance on snacks and attempt to sneak food into her room, will minimize the consequence of hoarding/sneaking food, and physically withdraw/avoid any attempt to discuss the topic/health related concerns. This behavior involves nesting, hoarding, and belief that Jennifer must protect her territory and belongings.<br><br>**Frequency:** Daily. Per parent report Jennifer's adult weight has varied over the past four years between 220 and 265 pounds. Largely depends on access to food and exercise. |

**Severity:** Chronic weight gain is medically associated with poor health, particularly with increased age. The food restriction helps decrease this risk. Consequences to date include complaints of food theft and the subsequent disruption of social networks, and the vacillation of weight with the subsequent negative attention received for apparent causes.

## Challenging Behavior #2 – Refusal to take care of Hygiene & Self-Care

**Definition:** Jennifer will often refuse to participate in community outings or complete activities of daily living, such as hygiene, laundry and other household tasks. Jennifer also refuses medical directions from her physicians, such as walking. When refusing to a request made by others, Jennifer makes verbal threats to assault staff or housemates. Responses include statements such as, "I am an adult, you can't tell me what to do" or refuses to leave a room and/or withdraws from the conversation.

**Frequency:** Daily. Largely depends on discrepancy between self-willed actions and externally identified expectations and/or requests.

**Severity:** If Jennifer refuses medical directives, this could be detrimental to her health. If verbal threats occur, they generally are not severe, but if staff or other clients were unaware of what is happening they could be injured if Jennifer followed through with the threat of assaulting others. Consequences to date include poor hygiene, poor eating habits, diminished health, disruption in social networks, prolonged environmental tensions that interfere with housing stability and housemate functioning, and heightened sensitivity to offense by subsequent interactions.

## Challenging Behavior #3 – Picking (Trichotillomania Disorder)

**Definition:** Jennifer will often pick her skin, pick at a wound, or pull out her hair.

**Frequency:** At least once a week. Largely depends on environmental stressors, housemate behaviors, and intensity/duration of stressor.

**Severity :** Poses a severe health risk in that the site of picking could become infected if not properly monitored. Consequences occurred to date include open wounds and physical discomfort.

## Challenging Behavior #4 – Verbal Aggression

**Definition:** Jennifer may scream, yell or swear at roommates or staff.
**Frequency:** Varies. Has the potential to become more frequent depending on staff/housemate responses, consistency in support, and perceived respect and/or control.

**Severity :** If staff are able to redirect Jennifer the risk to staff or others is minimal. If not, the risk could be significant. Consequences occurred to date include emotional distress, disrupted social networks, prolonged environmental tensions that interfere with housing stability and housemate functioning, and heightened sensitivity to offense by subsequent interactions.

## Challenging Behavior #5 – Physical Aggression

**Definition:** Jennifer may swing her fists, smack or hit an individual she is upset with or pick up an object and throw it, causing it to break. Jennifer may also slam doors when she is upset.

**Frequency:** Varies. Has the potential to become more frequent depending on staff/housemate responses, consistency in support, and perceived respect and/or control. **Severity :** If staff are able to redirect Jennifer the risk to staff or others is minimal. If not, the risk could be significant. Consequences occurred to date include emotional distress, disrupted social networks, physical discomfort, heightened sensitivity to offense by subsequent interactions, and risks of police involvement.

## DATA ANALYSIS / FUNCTIONAL ASSESSMENT PROCEDURES:

Procedures: This information was gathered from conversations with Jennifer's parents and with staff who have experience working with Jennifer since she entered the Agency program and a review of Jennifer's records.

### Behavior #1: Food Theft or Bingeing

Antecedents (Setting Events & Predictors):

· Jennifer has an impulse control disorder and this likely plays a key role in her food intake.

· If food is left unlocked or available without supervision it will prompt her to steal food.

- Jennifer expresses anger regarding her food restrictions and reacts toward this. restriction with a lot of defiance and negativity towards those imposing the restriction.

- Grocery Shopping.
- Allowance funds from the week's check are still available.
- Peers are currently eating/snacking.
- Visits in the community where food is not secured.
- Hanging out in locations where food is available (i.e., mall food courts, friend's house, etc.).

Consequence (Function):

- Food binging and hoarding has clinically been found to be associated with decrease in feelings of anxiety and feelings of depression as well as escaping negative feelings.
- Food binging and hoarding has also been clinically associated with feelings of fullness and the positive feelings of physical satiety, relative calm, satiation, and sleepiness; all of which may contribute reinforcement.

**SUMMARY STATEMENTS:**

Jennifer is on a physician restricted 1800 calorie per day diet. Given the opportunity (lack of supervision from staff, or if the cupboard or refrigerator is left unlocked, or housemates offer food), Jennifer will eat large quantities of food as well as hoard food.

**Overview:**

Jennifer is likely to engage is Food Theft & Binging when in the community or food is left accessible in the house without supervision so that she can obtain food and store in her room for later snacking/satisfy craving. This behavior is more likely to occur when out of staff sight, when in the community, with visiting family, when JDP classes, when at community functions, etc.

This behavior is less likely to occur when supervised by staff, when others responsible for her care are aware of her issues with food, when food is secured in the house, etc. It does not appear that it is relieving hunger, as nutritious meals and snacks are available and offered by staff throughout the day. It is possible that it may be a compulsive issue or a desire to be more independent (unsafe microwave use, eating raw meats, etc. rather than asking for staff assistance).

**Behavior #2: Refusal to take care of Hygiene & Self-Care**

Antecedents (Setting Events & Predictors):

- Being told to do something.
- Being told that she cannot do something.

- Lack of quality sleep or rest.
- Irritability.
- Perceived offense and/or disrespect.
- Feeling manipulated and/or bullied.
- Feeling a request is unfair, and limiting of her choice/rights.

- Belief that another's request/description is inconsistent with her self/world view.

- Change in access to desired items (i.e., food, etc.) in contrast to prior timeframe (whether access was acquired legitimately or not).

Consequence (Function):

- To Escape an unwanted request and/or to make something (person or event) stop that is upsetting her and feel in control.

- To feel more independent and assert control over a situation she is unhappy with.

**SUMMARY STATEMENTS:**

At this stage Jennifer will say she already did something in order to get out of it, say she will do it later but then later still not follow through, or refuse directly.

At this stage Jennifer will usually refuse openly then go into her bedroom, slamming her door behind her.

**Overview-**

Jennifer is likely to refuse to take care of her hygiene and self-care when she is engaged in a power struggle, irritable, or sensitive to feedback so that she can obtain a sense of independence and control over the situation. This behavior is more likely to occur early in the morning right when she awakes, when she is feeling disrespected, etc.

This behavior is less likely to occur when staff give her the opportunity to take care of her self-care needs and them promptly report to staff, when given the opportunity to establish her own schedule for follow through, when the task is connected to preparing for an activity or visit in the community, etc.

**Behavior #3: Picking (Trichotillomania)**

Antecedents (Setting Events & Predictors):

- Negative self-image

- Opportunity (lack of supervision)

- Seeking attention from staff

- Inactivity

- Shower time or daily hygiene routine

- Performance pressures

- Strong urge to "pull" or "pick"

- Frustration, Worry, Anxiety

<u>Consequence (Function):</u>

- To Release of pain relieving endorphins
- To Decrease in tension/anxiety/negative feelings.

## SUMMARY STATEMENTS:

At this stage Jennifer will pick at her skin or hair in private, usually while in her bedroom.

## Overview-

Jennifer is likely to engage in trichotillomania when overwhelmed by perceived social pressures, when fearful of consequences for what she believes will be poor performance, when talking about sensitive issues, and when feeling acutely sensitive to feedback in an effort to help her self-regulate acute anxiety, decrease her anxiety, and instill a sense of calm and control over how she responds to a situation. This behavior is more likely to occur when discussing sensitive topics and is subsequently isolative and unsupervised in her.

This behavior is less likely to occur when staff talk to Jennifer about picking, when her environment provides an opportunity to distract/redirect/and more properly self-regulate tension, and when social pressures are minimal/attempt to collaborate more so than direct.

## Behavior #4: Verbal Aggression

<u>Antecedents (Setting Events & Predictors):</u>

- Seeking attention from staff
- Inability to express her needs or wants verbally

- Being told that she cannot do something

- A peer expresses a viewpoint that is discrepant with her own self/world view

- The belief that this means she has done something wrong, is bad, etc.

- Belief that she is not being listened to

- Perception that she is not being respected

- Perception that the outcome is a contest of stamina, voice, tone, volume, etc.

Consequence (Function):

- To Gain attention of someone (could be staff, parents, etc.)

- To push others away

- To get what she wants or escape the experience of being controlled by others

**SUMMARY STATEMENTS:**

When Jennifer becomes frustrated she may use yelling and swearing to attempt to stop or avoid the situation, to dominate a discussion and have her opinion heard/dominate/triumph, and otherwise assert herself.

If the situation that is bothering her does not stop, or she does not get an immediate response and help from staff to assist her to avoid the situation, she may further escalate to physical aggression depending on duration, intensity, stress-threshold at the moment, personal boundaries, and proximity to the stimulus.

**Overview:**

Jennifer is likely to engage in verbal aggression when in conflict with peers about how things should be done, when feeling disrespected, when feeling that she will not be treated respectfully so that she can impose her opinion on others through the persuasion of force, push others away so that she doesn't have to address the situation any longer, etc. . This behavior is more likely to occur in dramatic escalated settings that involve peers or when issues present that directly conflict with her belief (i.e., food, diet, and weight), etc.

This behavior is less likely to occur when peers & staff use a calm modulated tone, when the words used are respectful and neutral, when sympathy of her position can be displayed, when her beliefs can be validated and/or paraphrased as reasonable, etc.

**Behavior #5: Physical Aggression**

Antecedents (Setting Events & Predictors):

·   Inability to express her needs or wants verbally
·   Seeking attention from staff

·   Being told to do something

·   Being told that she cannot do something

·   Perception of offense

·   Perception that she is being attacked (i.e., physically and verbally) and needs to defend herself
·   Intrusion into her bedroom (historically by housemates)

Consequence (Function):

·   To express needs or wants.
·   To Ease her frustration

·   To make something (person or event) stop that is upsetting her

·   To retaliate, harm, or rectify the perception of wrongdoing

·   To assert the 'righteousness' or 'correctness' of her position/opinion

·   To gain control

**SUMMARY STATEMENTS:**

When frustrated Jennifer also presents great difficulty in walking away, being redirected, accepting staff support to intervene & restructure the interaction, or consider alternative viewpoints as valid. Jennifer's thinking becomes increasingly concrete, inflexible, static, and largely unresponsive to attempts at cognitive restructuring until calmed.

When Jennifer becomes frustrated she yells, frequently closes personal distance between others, asserts herself unilaterally and definitely, decrease collaborative approach to dialogue, may swing her fists, hit others, throw items, pull hair, push others, etc.

**Overview:**

Jennifer is likely to engage in physical aggression when she is physically attacked so that she can protect herself, retaliate in kind, or force others to accept her position and leave her alone. This behavior is more likely to occur during a heated argument with others familiar to her, within close physical proximity.

This behavior is less likely to occur when staff can help set the tone for the conversation, establish boundaries and limit setting, when staff can redirect to more useful skills to address the escalation, and when Jennifer feels safe, etc. There are no known reports of Jennifer hitting staff.

**Positive Behavior Support Plan (PBSP)**

**PREVENTION STRATEGIES:**

**Environmental:**

· ***Staff is to plan according to the environment's access to food as frequently as is possible - in an effort to insure that food is not accessible. By avoiding access to food in the first place there is no need for a

> 1) post hoc response to subsequent unsuccessful attempts to gain access to food,
> 2) follow up discussion about the successful acquisition of food (that was not avoided by preplanning),
> 3) or the subsequent stigmatization of the dietary guidelines as a negative (versus positive) opportunity to feel & be healthy.

· Jennifer will have restricted access to food and is on an 1800 calorie per day diet per her primary care doctor.

· She will be provided the opportunity to consume three meals a day with a nutritious snack in the mid-morning and midafternoon.
· Staff will offer healthy options for snacking

· Staff will assist the housemates to develop a shopping list; monitoring it for minimal finger foods, junk foods, etc.; placing emphasis on healthy foods that are natural and/or need preparation.

· Staff will seek to cash the weekly allowance check at a bank, instead of at the store as much as possible, in an effort to avoid purchases of food versus non-food items
· When planning Jennifer's day, change and flexibility should be built into the schedule; allowing for change in mood, variations in stress tolerance, etc.

· Staff will document picking on a daily basis.

· Staff will check Jennifer for sores or wounds and record findings daily.

**Psychosocial/Interpersonal:**

- Jennifer's participation in JDP classes and activities will be encouraged regularly. Jennifer currently enjoys attending art class on Mondays and socialization class on Thursdays.

- Jennifer will be encouraged to participate in all medication management appointments a well as appointments with her primary care doctor on a regular basis.
- Staff is to plan outings in advance, preferably at a weekly house meeting with the household, with Jennifer's assistance that she would enjoy in participating in.

## Intrapersonal:

- Staff are to make a point of modeling appropriate social interactions as well as diet

- Whenever practical, staff should respond quickly and in a positive manner to any reasonable request for attention (or for a course of action) put forward by Jennifer.

## TEACHING AND TRAINING SUPPORTS:

***Several core strategies are recommended for both training and intervention supports:

- Staff is to utilize reflective listening, coaching, and collaborative planning methods to build upon Jennifer's interests and strengths.

- Staff is to help Jennifer to plan strategies, identify resources, and implement schedules that help introduce a routine, structure, consistency, and predictability in Jennifer's routine.

- Staff is to support Jennifer to seek out new opportunities based on current interests; the process is to be collaborative, inquisitive, and reinforcing of existing strengths and interests.

***Staff is to respond to refusals or resistance with:

- Reflective listening, helping Jennifer identify her priorities and the consequences of prioritizing her way, helping her identify conflicts in her priorities and thereby re-prioritize,

- Helping Jennifer to identify her known values, interests, and priorities in an effort to align her current prioritization of interests with a healthier, fairer, and more strength based plan/strategy,

By planning in advance (and thus avoiding the natural resistance that often comes with unexpected changes), and role modeling an equitable/balanced empathy and compassion with the group whom she may be in conflict with.

**Staff is to continue to support Jennifer with developing problem solving skills by:**

- Helping Jennifer problem solve an outcome if an activity is cancelled or postponed. Let her know the problem and have her help you solve it. For example: Staff will contact the organization to find out what happened, why they did not show up, etc.?

- Helping Jennifer learn positive communication techniques by:

- Making communication part of the solution. When problems do arise, staff should seek understanding first.

- Approaching the situation or conflict on a positive manner and use "I" statements (for example, "Jennifer what I hear you saying is…"

- Using questions to invite solutions to the problem. For example, staff could say, "What can we do together to solve the problem?"

- Allowing for a break or a change in discussion if Jennifer begins to become more frustrated by the conversation (Jennifer may like to retreat to her room for a short period of time to de-escalate or call her grandmother. Staff could also encourage her to count to ten or complete beep breathing exercises.)

- Offering Jennifer the option to create a list of frustrations If she doesn't feel like "talking" about the problem

- Actively helping Jennifer brainstorm ideas for possible solutions without judgment

- Once a list of solutions has been developed, together staff and Jennifer should pick out the best solution to the problem (keeping in mind it may be beneficial to have a back-up plan/solution)

- After the conflict/problem is over, it would be beneficial for staff and Jennifer to discuss how the decision making process worked out and discuss whether or not any changes need to be made to the plan should the same conflict arise again.

**Staff is to continue to support Jennifer in developing age appropriate relationships, to include housemates. Staff can support Jennifer by:**

***Communicating: 1) the importance of making sure she is safe, 2) that that she is communicating her boundaries and expectations clearly, 3) not to accept anything from a stranger, 4) that it is unsafe to go anywhere with someone she does not know, 5) that if she is uncomfortable with someone's comments or behaviors she should tell staff right away.

***Discussing: 1) her current relationship(s); a) nature, b) expectations, c) characteristics/ history of the person she is 'dating', d) where she knows/sees this person, e) plans (if implied), 2) how to stay safe.

☐ Encouraging her to participate in social activities such as the dances/outings/picnics, and other activities offered through the community.

☐ Creating a list of activities with Jennifer that is important to her in hopes of encouraging participation in those activities so that she can meet peers with common interests.

☐ Assisting with integrating and acceptance in social situations.

Staff may do this by role modeling appropriate social interactions while in the community.

For example, if staff and Jennifer arrive at an event (Dance for example), staff could model appropriate social skills by saying "Hello, how are you today?" to a fellow participant as a way to begin a conversation. Once the conversation has begun, staff can introduce Jennifer to the peer if he already has not done so.

If the conversation is about the dance for example, staff could ask the participant what their favorite type of music is. Hopefully that will create an opportunity for Jennifer to begin to discuss her musical interests and begin to form a "common ground" that would allow for the conversation and hopefully a friendship begin.

**Staff are to facilitate Jennifer's self- esteem by:**

***Identify opportunities that Jennifer can engage in where she will be successful; this also includes avoiding situations where Jennifer is going to feel a loss of control/success

☐ Providing positive reinforcement of incremental functional behaviors.

☐ Refraining from comparing her to others.

☐ Offer choices rather than demands. The hope is to present the choice to Jennifer in a positive manner that will allow her to feel that it will be beneficial to her.

☐ Setting aside time every day for Jennifer to sit down with a trusted staff person of her choice to reflect on anything Jennifer wants to discuss.

☐ Staff is to show Jennifer they will listen. For example, "Calm down. Calm down. I'm listening. I'm listening"

## STRATEGIES FOR RESPONDING TO CHALLENGING BEHAVIORS:

\*\*\*Several core strategies are recommended for both training and intervention supports:

☐ Staff is to utilize reflective listening, coaching, and collaborative planning methods to build upon Jennifer's interests and strengths.

☐ Staff is to help Jennifer to plan strategies, identify resources, and implement schedules that help introduce a routine, structure, consistency, and predictability in Jennifer's routine.

☐ Staff is to support Jennifer to seek out new opportunities based on current interests; the process is to be collaborative, inquisitive, and reinforcing of existing strengths and interests.

\*\*\*Staff is to respond to refusals or resistance with:

    ☐ Reflective listening, helping Jennifer identify her priorities and the consequences of prioritizing her way, helping her identify conflicts in her priorities and thereby re-prioritize,

    ☐ Helping Jennifer to identify her known values, interests, and priorities in an effort to align her current prioritization of interests with a healthier, fairer, and more strength based plan/strategy,

    ☐ By planning in advance (and thus avoiding the natural resistance that often comes with unexpected changes), and role modeling an equitable/balanced empathy and compassion with the group whom she may be in conflict with.

### Behavior #1: Food Hoarding & Binging

☐ \*\*\*Jennifer is to be given the opportunity to:
    Participate in healthy food preparation (meal planning, using the microwave and learning to cook) if she desires.
    Staff is to collaboratively plan meals with Jennifer that are healthy, balanced, and items that she enjoys.

    Jennifer enjoys eating healthy as well as unhealthy foods. By introducing healthy items that Jennifer enjoys she will be less likely to experience the diet as a restriction and more as an opportunity to eat things that are enjoyable but not detrimental to her health.

Staff is to provide social reinforcement to Jennifer for eating healthy, selecting healthy choices, taking care of her health, her displayed knowledge of health and nutrition, and her accomplishments while working on having a healthy lifestyle.

- For food hoarding or binging, ensure that the kitchen is locked up and secure.
- Staff is to be present when unloading groceries upon returning from grocery shopping to ensure that Jennifer does not take food items to her room.
- Food is to be guarded at all times. A doctor's order is in place to authorize locking the fridge and pantry.

- Staff is to clean Jennifer's room when she is in the community and when on leave visiting family.

- Staff is to document daily food intake on the food tracking form. Staff is to document breakfast, lunch, snack, dinner; portion size and calories.
- Staff is to create a meal plan for the following week a week in advance specifying each meal's content. Staff is to design these meals according to the Recommended Daily Allowance (RDA) for each food group.

**The following have been observed environmental antecedents leading to increased access to sneaking and hoarding food:**

- Issue: Report that Jennifer is getting food when she is going out to her volunteer job. This would be with her $10.00 weekly allowance. Strategy: Staff will continue to collaborate with the job developer surrounding attempts to gain access to food while out in the community/attending her volunteer job. *Staff will identify environments where food can be accessed and plan accordingly.

- Issue: In the past, Weekly allowance checks have been getting cashed at the customer service desk of Safeway for convenience. Strategy: For times when staff have the van, which is the preference for shopping (and cashing checks), staff will be asked to go to a bank and then elsewhere to spend the bulk if not all of the money before going shopping. This should result in less compulsive spending on food right at the moment when the check is cashed & spends some of the money before her volunteer job two days later.

- Issue: Jennifer goes to JDP for groups & other services up to twice a week. During these times she is observed frequently going into the bathroom and other areas male staff cannot follow, to apparently snack on food. Strategy: Staff will plan accordingly including working with Jennifer to bring a healthy snack to JDP, not eating immediately before going to JDP in an effort to properly regulate caloric intake if she is observed snacking and/or binging at JDP in secret, etc.

**Behavior #2: Refusal to take care of Hygiene or Self-Care**

☐ Staff is to help Jennifer distinguish between bad choice and bad person
☐ Staff is to help Jennifer distinguish between learning and being wrong
☐ Staff is to help Jennifer distinguish between being disrespectful and someone having overreacted to a situation
☐ Staff is to help Jennifer distinguish their supportive role and that of others who are involved in her care.
☐ Staff is to help Jennifer distinguish the difference between having the options inherent in choice and her perception of being told what to do.
☐ Staff is to help Jennifer distinguish between effective & ineffective communication styles currently in her repertoire
☐ Staff is to help Jennifer emphasize how certain behaviors influence different outcomes, good & bad, using Jennifer's system of evaluation and goals desired
☐ Staff is to help Jennifer identify what her priorities are, what outcomes she is looking for, evaluate if her approach is getting her needs med, and help problem solve alternatives when her needs are not getting med
☐ Staff is to provide Jennifer with positive reinforcement when she completes her daily hygiene routine or puts on a nice outfit or does her hair or paints her fingernails, etc.

☐ Staff is to create an activity plan for each day of the oncoming week using the desk calendar. Staff is to document in the OGN's the duration of the activity, type of activity, and/or if it was refused.

**Behavior #3: Picking**

☐ A trusted female staff will check Jennifer for sores or wounds daily.
☐ If Jennifer is isolating herself in her room, she should be routinely checked to ensure that she is not picking her skin or pulling her hair.

☐ Assist Jennifer with her personal hygiene and appearance.

☐ Offer to go shopping for nail polish or hair accessories, etc. to help her feel more positive about her body image and appearance.

**Behavior #4: Verbal Aggression:**

☐ Attend to appropriate interactions: Speak to Jennifer in a matter-of-fact tone of voice and inform her that you will discuss her wish when her voice is calm.

- Attempt to redirect Jennifer. Explain to Jennifer that it's clear that she is upset and offer to talk as soon as she is ready to do so.
- Intervene, structuring the conversation so that it is directed towards "I" statements, labeling one's own feelings, avoids blaming & labels, and validates viewpoints.

## Behavior #5: Physical Aggression:

- If Jennifer's agitation persists to the point where threats of violence occur or actual violence occurs deflect any further attempts by positioning yourself out of harm's way or between Jennifer and the peer housemate to provide a visual barrier. Give the directive: "Jennifer, Stop, I can't let you hurt _____."
  - Employ appropriate CPI techniques, if necessary. Provide instruction by stating "I'll talk with you when you are calm."
  - Ignore inappropriate attention-seeking behaviors if possible.

- When Jennifer is verbally aggressive, quickly assess the environment to see if a peer is likely to be upset by or respond aggressively to Jennifer's loud, verbal outbursts.
  - Provide protection, as necessary, and instruct peers to simply ignore the behavior or suggest that they move to an area where they may be more comfortable.
  - Let Jennifer know that you would like to talk with her but only if she can do so in a calm voice. Ignore all further verbal outbursts.
- Staff can call the on-call pager (Crisis Stabilization Team) for guidance and assistance
- Call 911 if at any time you are in danger or other individuals/roommates are in danger of being hurt by Jennifer or if Jennifer is in danger of hurting herself.

## DATA COLLECTION AND MONITORING:

Goals:

0 occurrences of food theft or binging

0 occurrences of isolation of self

0 occurrences of non-compliance

0 occurrences of obsessive compulsive behavior

0 occurrences of verbal aggression

0 occurrences of physical aggression

Jennifer will continue working on challenging behaviors with her JDP Counselor

Jennifer's staff will track any issues/concerns that they might have (as well as outbursts or incidents) on the Counseling Notes as well as in her on-going narratives and address any concerns on a program concern form. The Program Director and staff will monitor progress in the monthly summaries and attend quarterly meetings with the treatment team (assigned case manager and JDP case manager to discuss any changes).

**Documentation**: The staff will document all information on any types of behaviors noting any behavior that is different from Jennifer's baseline behaviors. If Jennifer is experiencing any type of behavior that is listed above or if an incident has taken place, the staff would document in the On-Going Narrative and Incident Report Form. However, if the behavior appears to warrant any type of medical or mental health intervention, the staff must document in the On-Going Narrative, The Green Medical Incident Log in the client's medical book and then on the Medical or Mental Health Appointment Sheet. The staff will check the client's Psychoactive medication plans to look for any type of side effect symptoms, notifying the Program Director and scheduling an appointment with the provider as soon as possible.

**Success** : All and any positive changes in negative behavioral issues will be considered a success.

**Monitoring**: The Program Director will monitor Jennifer's plan and progression weekly at shift changes and address any issues with staff. The Program Director will also meet quarterly with the case manager, vocational provider and assigned case manager to discuss issues or progress or concerns that Jennifer or her staff may have.

# RECOMMENDED GUIDELINES FOR DEVELOPING

# FUNCTIONAL ASSESSMENTS AND POSITIVE BEHAVIOR SUPPORT PLANS

Source: POSITIVE BEHAVIOR SUPPORT POLICY, § 5.14 (Washington State Department Departmental Disabilities Administration 2015).

This section includes guidelines for writing positive behavior support plans, and conducting functional behavior assessment (which are used to develop the PBSP). These guidelines are borrowed from the DDA 5.14 legislation in Washington State, and so represent an example of how significantly the PBS methodology has been embraced

These guidelines are intended to assist people who conduct functional assessments (FA) and develop positive behavior support plans (PBSP) for individuals with challenging behaviors. The guidelines describe the type of information that should be included in a written FA and PBSP.

Some professionals use the terms "functional analysis" and "functional behavioral assessment." For the purpose of these guidelines, these mean the same as "functional assessment."

## FUNCTIONAL ASSESSMENT (FA)

The format for the written FA is flexible regarding where the information listed below is entered, especially if a different organization leads to a more concise and understandable rationale. However, all FAs must contain these four major sections with these headings:

- ☐ *Description and Pertinent History;*
- ☐ *Definition of Challenging Behavior(s);*
- ☐ *Data Analysis/Assessment Procedures; and*
- ☐ *Summary Statements.*

### Description and Pertinent History

- ☐ Briefly describe the person to help the reader understand the "whole person" and not just the person's challenging behavior. The reader should understand the positive qualities of the person, and not just see them as a group of problem behaviors.

"Pertinent" history means 1) information that assists in understanding the development of the challenging behaviors (e.g., traumatic events; family history of psychiatric disorders that may create a predisposition to psychiatric problems; genetic conditions known to predict certain behaviors); and 2) information that identifies potential setting events and/or antecedents to the challenging behaviors (e.g., diabetes sets the stage for food-related behavioral issues; communication deficits helped create a situation where the challenging behaviors became the most effective way to get what the person wanted). The setting event and antecedent factors identified in "pertinent history" need to be summarized in the A-B-C model in the Data Analysis and Summary Statement sections.

☐ List abilities (strengths) and disability conditions.

  ☐ Briefly describe the person's cognitive, adaptive and emotional functioning when the person is doing well.

☐ List interests, activities, and hobbies. Refer the reader to a Person Centered Plan for more detail, if one exists.
  ☐ Pertinent life experiences that may impact current behaviors.
  ☐ Estimate how well the person's current life meets their wishes and needs.

☐ List current medical and psychiatric conditions. List current diagnoses and medications. When the collected information has conflicting diagnoses, make sure that you are using those of the current treating professional. The diagnoses contained in the FA should be consistent with the client's other plans (e.g., Cross System Crisis Plan, Individual Support Plan).

☐ If requesting to use restrictive procedures, describe why less restrictive methods are not sufficient.

**Definition of Challenging Behavior(s)**

☐ Describe each behavior of concern separately unless you are defining a consistent grouping, such as delusions.

☐ List frequency, duration, and severity/intensity of the behavior based on the best available data (severity = risks to person and others).

## Data Analysis/Assessment Procedures

☐ List how the data was collected for the assessment (e.g., structured and informal interviews, observations, record reviews, scatter plots, etc.).

☐ Describe the data and how it fits with the **A-B-C** model:

*Antecedents (Setting Events and Predictors)* → *Behavior* → *Consequence (Function)*

To describe the data, explain what was found with each data type collected (e.g., A-B-C observation, scatterplot analysis, FA interview). Recounting incidents that show the A-B-C pattern is suggested.

☐ List the setting events and predictors/antecedents identified through the analysis of collected information and the behavior(s) and consequences (functions) to which those setting events and predictors relate.

☐ List specific medical, psychiatric and quality of life problems that appear to be setting events or predictors.

☐ If the same behavior serves more than one function, identify which factors predict which function is being served.

☐ Assess and list the setting events or predictors for the positive, prosocial behavior that the person exhibits as one basis for designing preventive interventions (by increasing those positive events).

## Summary Statements

☐ <u>Summarize the FA with the best hypothesis (i.e., reason or purpose) why the person engages in the behavior</u>. Describe the typical relationship between the setting events/predictors and the behavior. One way to construct a summary statement is:

*When Predictor X occurs, Behavior Y is likely to occur so the person can obtain/avoid Consequence Z (the function). This behavior will be more likely to occur when setting events A, B, or C is present.*

☐ When there are multiple behaviors that do not appear to serve the same function for the person, include a summary statement for each behavior.

☐ When there are multiple functions identified for a single behavior, you may want to write separate summary statements for the different setting events and/or predictors. One example is:

> *When asked to do chores like take his dirty clothes to the laundry room or take his dishes to the kitchen after meals, hitting himself serves the purpose of escaping those requests as staff doesn't want to see more self-injury. At other times, when his favorite staff is busy helping others, he may hit himself to try to regain their attention.*

# POSITIVE BEHAVIOR SUPPORT PLAN (PBSP)

It is recommended that the FA and PBSP be two distinct documents. If you are writing the FA and PBSP as separate documents, start the PBSP with a recap of the *Behavioral Definitions* and the *Summary Statements* from the FA so that the reader will understand the rationale for the procedures in the PBSP. If you are including both the FA and PBSP in one document, start below. Keep instructions clear, concise, and let the reader know exactly what actions they should take. All PBSPs must contain these four major sections with these headings:

- ☐ Prevention Strategies;

- ☐ Teaching/Training Supports;
- ☐ Strategies for Responding to Challenging Behaviors; and

- ☐ Data Collection and Monitoring.

## Prevention Strategies

The goal in writing prevention strategies is to address major deficiencies in quality of life factors (i.e., deficiencies in power and choice, community integration, status, relationships, competence, health, and safety) and each setting event/predictor identified by the FA.

Prevention strategies try to avoid the setting events/predictors that occur prior to the challenging behavior, or to minimize their occurrence and impact when they can't be avoided. Strategies might also be developed to modify the antecedents so they do not predict the challenging behavior. These strategies should be specific, measurable actions that staff or caregivers can do (i.e., not just general ideas).

- ☐ **Environmental** - Changes in the person's environment to avoid, modify, or minimize antecedents/predictors identified in the FA.

- ☐ **Psychosocial /Interpersonal** - More general changes that improve the quality of the person's life and promote obtaining more natural reinforcers via relationships, integration, power and choice, competence, and status or dignity.

  - ☐ List needed changes in the person's life, even if they cannot be achieved right away. Tie these identified needs into the broader Person Centered Plan.

☐ **Intrapersonal** - Medical, psychological, and/or psychiatric interventions that address setting events/predictors identified in the FA.

## Teaching/Training Supports

☐ Define and list teaching and reinforcement procedures (if not covered under *Prevention Strategies*) to improve general skills that will allow the person to access important reinforcers or lifestyle outcomes and reduce the person's need to use challenging behaviors; <u>and</u>

☐ Define and list procedures to teach and reinforce specific behaviors that can serve as a replacement behavior (i.e., an appropriate behavior that achieves the same function for the person as the challenging behavior). Clearly list staff or caregiver behaviors that will teach, prompt and reinforce the use of this replacement behavior; <u>or</u>

☐ If the person has these skills already, list staff or caregiver behaviors to reinforce the appropriate replacement behavior(s) so that they will be used while minimizing or stopping reinforcement for the challenging behavior(s).

## Strategies for Responding to Challenging Behaviors

☐ List specific actions that staff or caregivers should take when reacting to each challenging behavior (there may be different responses, depending on the behavior):

   ☐ To ensure protection.

   ☐ To redirect, distract, etc.

   ☐ To help the person problem solve.
   ☐ To prompt the use of the replacement or alternate behaviors, if possible, and steps to reinforce using those appropriate behaviors.
   ☐ To avoid or minimize reinforcement of the challenging behaviors.

☐ If implementing a restrictive procedure, clearly describe the specific procedure(s) and provide directions for implementing the procedure(s).

## Consistency with the Cross Systems Crisis Plan (CSCP)

☐ If there is a Cross Systems Crisis Plan (CSCP) in place, make sure these steps are consistent with the CSCP.

☐ If there is not a CSCP or other crisis plan document, list in the PBSP the specific actions that staff or caregivers are to take prior to/during a crisis to ensure protection and request assistance from internal and external resources (e.g., staff supervisor, police, DDA).

## Data Collection and Monitoring

☐ Operationally define the goals of the PBSP in terms of specific, observable behaviors.

☐ Indicate what data is needed to evaluate success (i.e., frequency, duration, and severity/ intensity of the target behaviors, and increase in replacement behaviors).

☐ Provide instructions to staff or caregivers on how to collect this data (e.g., forms, charts, procedures).

☐ List who will monitor outcomes, need for revisions, and evaluate success and process for monitoring.

☐ Recommend displaying data in a graph over time for easy analysis.

# Concluding Remarks

The Positive Behavior Support model represents a robust and evidence based framework for supporting skill development and avoiding the need for counter-productive behaviors to be used. Less complex, and challenging, behaviors are addressed with the tools discussed in this book along with ongoing consultation with the care team members. More complex, and thus challenging, behaviors will benefit deeper exploration of the following tools in addition to the PBS framework:

- Applied Behavior Analysis (ABA)
- Functional Behavior Assessment (FBA)
- Behavioral Analysis Models (BA)
- Learning Development Models  (LD)
- Reinforcement Models
- Cognitive Behavioral Therapy (CB)
- Etc.

Each school of thought promotes their own tools, strategies, and processes to take center stage. Yet there is a general consensus among public and private advocates that the Positive Behavior Support framework should always be the first component considered when drafting a client support plan. Additional tools are often used in combination to increase the strength of the care team's analysis and insight into the behavior.

Because the PBS model is most often applied in the disabilities field the issue of cognition and insight frequently needs to be addressed first and foremost before identifying a support model.  This is where the power and insight of the ABA, FBA, and BA models are appreciated. Cognition is considered epiphenomena of behavior (a secondary effect or byproduct that arises from but does not causally influence a process, in particular).  Although many practitioners, and theorists, will argue the validity of this premise the ability to determine and evaluate causality based on observable (and thus behavioral) phenomena remains a significant strength of the behavioral models.

# Meal Planning Guide Book

The purpose of this guidebook is to provide caregivers a technical understanding of meal planning and the policy context in which meal planning is conducted.

## Legal Disclosure

This guidebook is not intended and should not be used as medical advice. Consult your primary care physician and nutritionist for specific instructions regarding nutrition, diets, or weight loss.

### Items you will need to implement a client centered meal plan

- Food Groups Basics, Mini Poster (found at: http://www.choosemyplate.gov/downloads/mini_poster_English_final.pdf )

- Meal Planning *Worksheet.*

- *Exception to Policy* document (ETP) ( health & nutrition issues).

- Physician's *Orders* (if they exist for h nutrition).

- Copy of the *Washington Administrat* (WAC) DDA policy 5.15 on restrictive for individuals with intellectual disak

- Recipe Book.

- Copy of a measurement chart for cooking

- *Notepad* for taking notes.

- *Positive Behavior Support Plan* (PBSP) if Health is a goal identified within the plan. Inclusion of this area in the PBSP is required if there is an ETP.

- *Individual Instruction & Support Plan* (IISP) if Health is a goal identified within the plan.

- *Meal Intake Worksheet* (optional).

- Notepad for documenting *grocery list.*

- *Client daily log* form (OGN, etc.).

# Food Groups Basics

- **What you need for this slide:** Food Groups Basics, Mini Poster.

- **The Groups:** Protein, Grains, Vegetables, Fruits, Dairy

- **Purpose:** To support health.

- **Goals:** Nutrition, weight, health, avoid illness, etc.

- **Strategies:** There are many types of diets. These are always supplemented with exercise.

_____

_____

_____

_____

_____

# Overview: Principles of Meal Planning

- Take inventory of what is already available in the house.

- Review recipe books for suggestions of what you would like to eat.

- Compare recipes identified with the inventory of food that you already have on hand.

- Prepare shopping list based on the items that still need to be purchased.

- Go Shopping!

- Store groceries, and label items if to be used exclusively for one meal(s) so they are not used in something else.

- Cook! Serve! Enjoy!

- Document intake

| Plan Steps | |
|---|---|
| | Inventory |
| | Recipes |
| | Compare to Inventory |
| | Shopping List |
| | Go Shopping |
| | Label |
| | Cook |
| | Intake |

# Meal Planning Worksheet

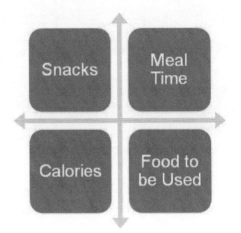

- **What you need for this slide:** Meal Planning Worksheet

- **Purpose**: Nutritional Meals.

- **Goals**: Identified in client plans and treatment documents.

- **Strategies**: Identified in client plans and treatment documents.

- **Exclusions**: Most restrictive strategies used cannot be used without proper medical documentation and approval from the Washington State Department of Developmental Disabilities.

_____

_____

_____

_____

_____

_____

# Exception to Policy (ETP) Document

- **What you need for this slide:** ETP for the clients you work with (if one exists)


- **Purpose:** Document template used to submit specific request to use restrictive procedures.

    o Must include history of the behavior

    o Must include history of strategies used to address this behavior, and ˙ ˙ ˙ ˙ ˙ ˙ ˙ ˙ ˙ those strategies.

    o Must include description ( used.

    o Must reference section of the behavior to be addres the sections exist

_____

# Physician's Orders

- **What you need for this slide:** The Physician's Orders for the clients you work with (if one exists).

- **Purpose:** Must state diagnosis to be treated by the strategies to be used. A physician's order is required for a request for an Exception to Policy (ETP) discussed in the previous slide.

  o Must state instructions in physician's own language.

  o Must state what specific strategies and methods are to be implemented.

  o Must be re-evaluated, written, and submitted every year with the Exception to Policy Request document.

_____

_____

_____

_____

_____

# Restrictions and the DDA Policy 5.15

http://www.dshs.wa.gov/pdf/adsa/DDA/policies/policy5.15.pdf

- **What you need for this slide:** Copy of the DDA Policy 5.15. (Quotations below)

- **"BACKGROUND:** When a client's behavior presents a threat of injury to self or others, or threatens significant damage to the property of others, steps must be taken to protect the client, others, or property from harm. It is expected that supports as described in the Division of Developmental Disabilities (DDA) Policy 5.14, *Positive Behavior Support,* will be used to lessen the behaviors and to eliminate the need for restrictive practices. When positive behavior support alone is insufficient, procedures that involve temporary restrictions to the client may be necessary (DDA policy 5.15)."

- **"PURPOSE:** This policy describes which restrictive procedures are allowed and which are prohibited, the circumstances under which allowed restrictive procedures may be used, the requirements that must be met before they may be used, and the requirements for documenting and monitoring their use (DDA policy 5.15. "

    - *"Note*: If the client understands and complies with his/her dietary restrictions (i.e., does not exhibit any challenging behaviors in response) and the client's food and kitchen/kitchen areas do not need to be secured, a PBSP is not required. For example, a person with diabetes who is on a special diet due to diabetes, but who complies willingly with the diet and for whom it is not necessary to lock up food or areas of the kitchen (DDA policy 5.15."

- **"Restrictive procedure** means a procedure that restricts a client's freedom of movement, restricts access to client property, requires a client to do something which he/she does not want to do, or removes something the client owns or has earned (DDA policy 5.15)."

_____

_____

_____

_____

_____

_____

_____

_____

"**Approval at the Regional Administrator Level: Is** required when a request is made to do the following:  a. Controlling food consumption for individuals who have behavioral issues (e.g., stealing food, running away to get food, being assaultive when denied food, etc.) related to unrestricted access to food when:

- A long-term threat exists to the client's health, as determined in writing by a physician; or

- A short-term threat exists (e.g., eating raw meat, uncontrolled intake of water, etc.); or

- It is necessary for assisting the client to live within his/her budget (DDA policy 5.15). "

- "**An ETP is required**: Whenever a client's food or kitchen is locked up and not accessible to the client without staff assistance (DDA policy 5.15). "

# Recipe Books

- **What you need for this slide:** Copies of Recipe Books that is available in your program & <u>measurement chart.</u>

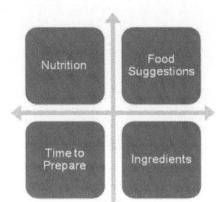

- **Purpose:** To aid staff creativity and of enjoyable variety for meals that the program.

- **Goals:** To support the specific food that are identified whether they ar nutritional, weight, intake related,

- **Strategies:** Recipe books, in partic...., ...... staff make nutritional meals. The caloric and nutritional values, time it takes to make the meal, and ingredients needed are all identified in each recipe.

- Recipe books can also be used in client discussions to evaluate what are nutritional foods, <u>nutritional choices</u>, and add <u>variety</u> to the week's meal planning so that the client is more invested in the goals the meal planning is intended to support.

_____

_____

_____

_____

_____

# Positive Behavior Support Plan (PBSP): Working with Challenging Behaviors

- **What you need for this slide:** Positive Behavior Support Plans for the clients you work with

- **PBSP History Section:** This section gives you a brief history of the client, behaviors, housing, family background, legal issues, etc.

- **PBSP Training Section:** This section identifies training strategies that are to be used to help the client develop effective skills (to replace challenging behaviors) to get their needs met.

- **PBSP Prevention Section:** This section identifies the interpersonal, intrapersonal, and environmental strategies that are to be used to help the client not resort to challenging behaviors.

- **PBSP Response Section:** This section identifies the strategies to be used when the challenging behaviors occur (and prevention was unsuccessful) (and when training of replacement behaviors was not effective for a/this specific situation).

- **PBSP Exception to Policy Section:** This section identifies the restrictive procedures that are approved (if any).

_____

_____

_____

_____

# Individual Instruction & Support Plan (IISP)

- **What you need for this slide:** IISP's for the clients you work with.

- **Purpose:** Goals are identified tha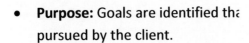 pursued by the client.

- **Goal:** Strategies are identified th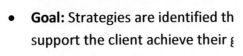 support the client achieve their g

- **Strategies:** Strategies are identif will use to support their own goal.

- **Keywords:** Keywords/language for the goal is identified that staff will use when writing the client daily log.

_____

_____

_____

_____

_____

# Meal Planning Intake Worksheet (optional)

- **What you need for this slide:** Copies of the meal planning intake worksheet (if one exists for the clients you work with).


- **Purpose:** To provide documentation of what is to be served.

- **Goal:** What is served is to be consistent with the physician's orders and the ETP document.

- **Strategies:** Are consistent with the strategies identified & explained in the positive behavior support plan.

- **Timing:** <u>Meal Planning</u> is always completed prior to <u>grocery shopping</u>, which is in turn always completed prior to <u>cooking & preparation</u>.

- **Factors Influencing Preference:** The quality of client's preferences for food is based on

  - 1) what is available,

  - 2) what is role modeled by staff,

  - 3) what is role modeled by peers,

  - 4) attitudes towards food (good or bad; healthy or unhealthy),

  - 5) attitudes towards one self (good or bad; attractive or unattractive), and

  - 6) culture (staying fit or appearing 'successful' by evidencing having access to lots of food).

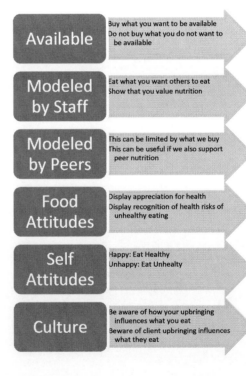

_____

_____

                                               -
_____

_____

# Client Daily Log Notes

- **What you need for this slide:** Copy of the document your program uses for daily log notes.

- **Purpose:** To help document and provide a record of the efforts, strategies, and the results of the services provided to support the client's goal.

- **Goal:** To help provide a record ( performance in pursuing their g

- **Strategies:**

  o The Exception to Policy ( identifies if there are an practices that are allowe

  o The Individual Instructio (IISP) identifies what is t pursuing, in their own la

  o The Positive Behavior Su identifies the strategies determined are best suited for this individual client to support them to achieve success.

  o The strategies from these documents are to be followed and can be used to describe staff efforts in the client's daily log.

_____

_____

_____

_____

# Developing the client support team

- **Purpose:** To insure the client has sufficient support to help them be successful and to insure that everyone is supporting the same goal(s).

- **Goal:** To support the goals identified in the physician's order, ETP, PBSP, IISP.

- **Strategies:** Solicit feedback from your team regularly. Provide information for discussion. Ask questions from your team. Plan around challenging areas. Tap the wisdom of the group. The more challenging the goal(s) the more regularly you should be communicating with the team.

_____

_____

_____

_____

_____

# Conclusions: Overview

- **Purpose:** Meal planning has many purposes. The general purpose of meal planning is to insure that healthy and nutritious meals are planned in advance. The structure provided by a pre-developed meal plan helps the staff to remain on track. It is also easier to keep a client focused on their goals when a meal plan is in place.

- **Goals:** Meal planning has many goals. The general goal of meal planning is nutrition, combatting/preventing illness, and increasing health.

- **Strategies:** Meal planning strategies depend on the 1) goal, the 2) client, the 3) team, the 4) physician's orders, and 5) the challenging behaviors. There is no on size meal plan that fits all of the different needs present in the larger client population we work with. Any 'cookie cutter' approach is likely to be unsuccessful.

_____

_____

_____

_____

_____

# Resources Online

http://www.dshs.wa.gov/pdf/adsa/DDA/policies/policy5.15.pdf

http://www.choosemyplate.gov/videos.html

http://www.choosemyplate.gov/food-groups/

http://www.nal.usda.gov/fnic/foodcomp/Bulletins/measurement_equivalents.html

http://www.jacn.org/content/24/2/83.full

## Post-Training Questions

1. Are all Meal Plans the same? Why?

2. Do all Meal Plans require an Exception to Policy? When do they?

3. What are the five food groups?

4. Where can you find the information to deal with the challenging behaviors that are seen when working around issues of food?

5. What documents will be able to tell you what the goals are for having a meal plan?

6. Arrange the following in the order of importance/use: A) shopping list, B) Meal plan, C) intake record, D) physician's order, E) PBSP, and F) Exception to Policy.

7. What types of skills might the training section of the PBSP seek to help the client develop?

| | |
|---|---|
| 1 tablespoon (tbsp) = | 3 teaspoons (tsp) |
| 1/16 cup (c) = | 1 tablespoon |
| 1/8 cup = | 2 tablespoons |
| 1/6 cup = | 2 tablespoons + 2 teaspoons |
| 1/4 cup = | 4 tablespoons |
| 1/3 cup = | 5 tablespoons + 1 teaspoon |
| 3/8 cup = | 6 tablespoons |
| 1/2 cup = | 8 tablespoons |
| 2/3 cup = | 10 tablespoons + 2 teaspoons |
| 3/4 cup = | 12 tablespoons |
| 1 cup = | 48 teaspoons |
| 1 cup= | 16 tablespoons |
| 8 fluid ounces (fl oz) = | 1 cup |
| 1 pint (pt) = | 2 cups |
| 1 quart (qt) = | 2 pints |
| 4 cups = | 1 quart |
| 1 gallon (gal) = | 4 quarts |
| 16 ounces (oz) = | 1 pound (lb) |
| 1 milliliter (ml) = | 1 cubic centimeter (cc) |
| 1 inch (in) = | 2.54 centimeters (cm) |

# Training Post-Test Answers

1. No. There are many diets. Different medical conditions justify different meal plans.

2. No. Only when there is a restriction to be implemented such as locking up the food, etc.

3. Protein, Grains, Dairy, Fruits, & Vegetables

4. Positive Behavior Support Plans: Training Section, Prevention Section, & Response Section.

5. Physician's Orders, ETP Form (if one is required), PBSP, and IISP

6. Physician's Order, Exception to Policy, PBSP, Shopping List, Meal Plan, and Intake Record.

7. Understanding nutrition, understanding weight loss, understanding portions, understanding the benefits of exercise, understanding how to exercise, understanding the risks associated with poor health, etc.

_ _ _ _ _ _ _ _ _ _ _ _ _ _ _ _ _ _ _ _ _ _ _ _ _ _ _ _ _ _ _ _ _ _ _ _ _ _ _ _ *Please return the questionnaire below to your training instructor or supervisor after completed. Your feedback is appreciated.*

## Post-Training Self-Evaluation

1. Did you find this training useful?                               Y          N

2. Did you find the way the information was presented to be helpful?      Y          N

3. Did you understand the information provided in this training?      Y          N

4. Do you believe you are now able to work with your team to implement meal planning in your program house?                               Y
      N

5. Did you find the combination of the video and the guidebook to help you learn the material presented?                               Y
      N

6. Would you suggest others to take this training?                       Y          N

# About the Author

Travis Barker was born in Seattle, Washington and moved to Vancouver, BC to found Innovate Vancouver, a business consulting and technology firm.

With over 20 years of experience in the public, social, and healthcare sectors, Travis Barker brings a wealth of experience and insight into project design, strategic planning, business culture, and the tools to support creativity and innovation.

Travis Barker completed his bachelor's degree in psychology, master's degree in public administration, post graduate certificate in project management, and an unfinished doctorate in organizational leadership (left to found a start-up).

Travis Barker can be reached at consulting@innovatevancouver.org or online at http://innovatevancouver.org

Printed in Great Britain
by Amazon